Preparing Your Heart for the High Holy Days

Preparing Your Heart for the High Holy Days

A Guided Journal

Kerry M. Olitzky and Rachel T. Sabath

With a Foreword by David Wolpe

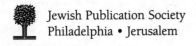

Jewish Publication Society
Philadelphia • Jerusalem

Designed by Sasgen Graphic Design, Philadelphia, PA

For those whom we have wronged—may we be forgiven.

Table of Contents

Foreword by David Wolpe ix

Acknowledgments xi

Sources   xiii

Introduction   xv

How to Use This Book xix

Elul 1

Tishrei: The Ten Days of Awe 63

Moving to Sukkot and Beyond 85

Teachers and Their Texts 93

Glossary   97

Foreword

Modern life discourages introspection. The demands upon us grow more insistent, and we run unceasingly through the swirl of events and person-alities that mark our lives. Most of us scrutinize ourselves only in extreme moments: times of trial or catastrophe. Rarely do we calmly resolve to hold a looking glass up to our own souls, eyes unwavering, and examine what we have done with our gifts, our obstacles, and our opportunities.

Yet spiritual teachers have always insisted that the tenor of life is deeply affected by these brief moments of serious self-examination. To pass through this world without knowing one's own soul is forever to carry a message unread. How can we know what we might accomplish without knowing the powers and temptation inside our own hearts?

According to the ancient rabbis, the purpose of all the *mitzvot* in the Jewish tradition is to "refine human beings" (Bereshit Rabbah, 44:1). That is, this vast, intricate tradition of commandments exists that we might begin to understand ourselves better, and refine our own souls. But none of us dwells alone. The world is a storehouse of souls. Therefore, most profoundly, Judaism is a system of *tikkun olam*, improving the world and all the souls in it, in the hope that they will carry their newfound knowl-edge into the family and marketplace. The single soul is humanity's most basic unit of promise; to better the individual soul carries hope for the fate of all.

Rosh Hashanah and Yom Kippur are the critical times in the Jewish year for self-examination. But many of us find it difficult to focus upon our inner selves at this time. Social concerns often override spiritual ones. In fact, the High Holy Days sometimes seem more about pageantry than prayer. At this time when our souls should be most exposed, we are often more concerned that our bodies be elaborately clothed. At this time when we should be most dedicated to renewing our commitments, we find it easier to renew acquaintances. We turn to small talk as a pleasant way to distract ourselves from the difficult excavation of past deeds and deep beliefs.

This book by Rabbis Kerry Olitzky and Rachel Sabath helps us focus ourselves on what is truly important. In these meditations the reader is given the chance to understand, and to grow. For a moment the din of the world is stilled. In these pages the melody of the single soul is revived. This work is a beautiful addition to the body of Jewish literature that helps us offer up more than set prayers and social graces. The authors remind us anew that, as the Talmud teaches: *Rachmana Liba Ba'aya*, God seeks the heart. ■

DAVID WOLPE

Acknowledgments

This volume grew out of a continuing desire to help fellow Jews embrace the spiritual rhythm of the Jewish calendar by focusing on specific periods, such as the *Elul–Tishrei* period, already designated by Jewish tradition as preparation time for the High Holy Days, as the holidays in this period have come to be known. This time span of forty days provides us with a spiritual map of sorts to help us find our way "back home." Therefore, our work as authors is much like that of cartographers, simply taking the routes that we have travelled and mapping them in an accessible format so that others might find their way as well. Each day that we are blessed to be alive, we continue on the journey.

We have many people to thank, for so many people have taught us the Torah of their lives so that we could bring these ideas together in one volume. This endeavor brought two people—teacher and student, now colleagues—together because of a mutual desire to kindle the spark in others by the flames burning in our individual souls. Knowing that the people at the Jewish Publication Society have joined us in our endeavor to find a spiritual center in the midst of Judaism is, in itself, extremely comforting. Dr. Ellen Frankel, an excellent editor and tremendous guide, has helped us to see even more direction in Jewish tradition than we ever thought possible. Without the support of students, teachers, and colleagues at Hebrew Union College-Jewish Institute of Religion, New York, none of this work would have been possible. The environment that we as a community have built there is a spiritual fountain from which we constantly draw strength and support. In addition, we want to thank the participants of the annual Morris Zimmerman Memorial Institute, as well as the regional Worship and Study Institutes, and the Consultations on the Respiritualization of the Synagogue, which are sponsored by HUC-JIR and are where many of these ideas were explored.

I want to express deep appreciation to Rabbi Michael Monson at the Jewish Publication Society. When we met more than ten years ago, we became friends overnight. I also want to thank my family. None of this work would have been possible without the support of Sheryl, Avi, and Jesse Olitzky.

K.M.O.

There have been a number of remarkable friends and colleagues who have stood near me and whose voices have echoed in my ears as this project emerged. I am grateful to Kerry for his invitation to build the *hevrutah*—the study partnership—which transformed and was transformed by this process. My parents, Suzanne Wells Sabath and Leon Sabath, have appreciated my uniqueness and consistently encouraged my growth. My two older sisters, Natasha and Joanna, have no less influenced me in this realm. A number of friends and colleagues have guided, challenged, and supported me: Joseph Edelheit, Steve Greenberg, Jonathan Huppert, Andrea London, Leon Morris, Yael Ridberg, Don Seeman, and Elana Zaiman. Yonatan Aumann, in particular, nourished me and helped me to prepare my heart as this book took shape. Above all, I am grateful to Eugene B. Borowitz and Nava Rephun who gave me courage and assured me that something of this *t'shuvah* might lead to more *t'shuvah*. ∎

R.T.S.

Sources

We have drawn on many traditional sources throughout this book: liturgy, particularly the traditional Ashkenazi *maḥzor* (prayer book of the High Holy Days); the Bible (in the 1985 JPS translation); rabbinic texts such as the Mishnah, Talmud, midrash, and codes; medieval ethical, mystical, and legal works; ḥasidic tales and teachings; and contemporary wisdom by such teachers as Abraham Joshua Heschel and Joseph Soloveitchik. Because this book is designed as an aid to meditation and reflection, we have chosen not to intrude with bibliographical references. By such omission, we mean no disrespect; rather, we are following an ancient Jewish oral tradition of citing teachings "in the name of" the teacher. ■

Introduction

During the High Holy Days period, Judaism draws us back to our community and to ourselves in a profoundly spiritual way, perhaps more forcefully than during any other time during the Jewish calendar year. On Rosh Hashanah and Yom Kippur, we find ourselves in the synagogue among thousands of other Jews in communities throughout the world struggling in a profound way to "come home" to Judaism, often after years of neglecting our religious heritage. We gather together as adults, but memories of childhood linger. Eagerly we try to recapture the more innocent moments of wonderment we may have experienced when we still lived under the protective care of our parents. Then we might have believed more naively that if we did the right thing, we would be forgiven; if not, we would be punished.

As we review our lives during the previous year and even further back, it may be difficult for us to find words to articulate the wide range of emotions that flood our minds. We all feel them in one way or another. We get together with family and friends where love may abound, but even here—or perhaps especially here—moments and memories of discord surface. We recognize the harsh realities of our lives: there are others whom we have chosen to exclude from our lives or, alternatively, others who have made personal choices to separate themselves from us. And death has taken the lives of many whom we have loved. Those whom we glimpse in the synagogue may remind us of those with whom we have established or avoided relationships during the year.

Letting Go of the Past

The period of Elul-Tishrei (the forty days leading up to Yom Kippur) is designed to help us let go of the pain in our past so we can embrace the future with hope. We can come together, feeling a sense of wholeness once again. There are both joy and pain mingled in these moments of self-reflection. We think back over where we have been in the past twelve months, how we got to this place in our lives, and where we had hoped to be. We may not be willing to admit it readily, but we yearn to experience a renewal of spirit. It's one of the many reasons we wait in such anxious anticipation for the High Holy Days throughout the summer. Rabbi Andrea Weiss teaches that the month of Elul serves as a special transitional moment, reflecting the traditional image of *bein hashamashot,* literally "between the suns." She suggests that Elul (late August, early September) is "a bridge between summer and fall, between long sunny days and crisp afternoons full of color and wind . . . between who we are and what we want to be; between regret and repentance, guilt and renewal; between the frustration of accepted patterns and the promise to change."

What is it that draws us in such large measure to our religious roots during this season? What brings us to the synagogue when we may not find ourselves such willing participants at other times of the year? Perhaps it is faith in God and our ability to change. Some of us may have found a private path for spirituality and at this time are looking to widen that path in the context of community. For even when we Jews engage in private prayer, we do so in the context of the people of Israel. It is the only way for us to function and survive as a people. Others among us yearn to recapture the sense of well-being we experienced in the synagogue of our childhood. As we grow older, such memories of our youth can bring us comfort. We recall the haunting notes of Kol Nidre that filled the synagogue. We remember waiting in eager anticipation to hear the shofar blast so that we could break our fasts. We think back, perhaps sheepishly, to our talking with our friends under the watchful eye of the rabbi. Some of us have none of these memories and seek to create them in our midst. Most of all, it is the promise of t'shuvah, the powerful possibility of repentance, renewal, and return, that affords us the opportunity to change the direction of our lives and reroute them. This is the religious force that drives us to the synagogue for the holidays. We may not have the vocabulary to communicate it exactly, but this desire to change cries out from our souls.

Our Relationship Beyond Self, With a Higher Self

We know we can't change, can't be transformed on our own. We recognize that our impulse to change arises out of the covenantal relationship our people established with God many generations ago, that is part of our people's ongoing attempt to make our lives sacred. We know that we are on a journey through the desert of our own lives. While this personal "God talk" might make some of us uncomfortable, we cannot deny its truth. The spirituality we seek so earnestly demands that we articulate our relationship with God, for it is our attempt to establish and maintain such a relationship that brings us an experience of the spiritual. Without such a relationship, spirituality becomes a word devoid of real meaning. This process can be meaningful even for those who doubt God's existence or doubt that they can have a relationship with God.

Perhaps you will have trouble with this aspect of the book, because the word "God" dredges up unpleasant or naive images from distant Hebrew school memories. You need no longer be bound to such memories.

Whatever you call this power beyond yourself, be it God or anything else, it is enough to recognize that something greater exists beyond us. Our tradition has come up with many names to call God. Choose a name that works for you so that you can step over this barrier to your own spiritual growth.

Our tradition suggests that the very name of the month of Elul is an acronym formed from the first letters of the well-known Song of Songs text, "_Ani l'dodi v'dodi li_" ("I am to my beloved and my beloved is mine"). The rabbis understood the Song of Songs—an erotic love poem in the Bible filled with nearness and distance, peace and conflict, yearning and fulfillment—to be an allegory reflecting the relationship between the individual and God. We return to the synagogue during the holidays to forge or affirm this relationship—a dynamic relationship of mutual dialogue between the individual and God that forms the basis for a sacred and holy life. Such a life does not come on its own, as we would like. We have to work for it. ■

How to Use This Book

How do we prepare for the spiritual renewal we long to experience? Rabbi Israel Salanter, the founder of the 19th century Musar movement, which stressed personal morality, kept totally silent during this forty-day period. He spoke to no one. In doing so, he was able to focus his entire attention on the repair of his inner self without any distraction. Some of his colleagues and disciples fasted (refrained from eating either completely or just during daylight hours). Most of us would find such intense measures quite foreign to our religious sensibilities. Instead we look for modes of preparation that fit our own spiritual style.

In the synagogue each Shabbat during Elul, the haftorahs of consolation, as they are called, are read, offering us comfort and compassion. Notably, these readings follow the fast of Tisha b'Av, which commemorates the destruction of the ancient Temples in Jerusalem. Not only do these prophetic readings mark real events in our history; they also speak directly to our own personal situations. Through the daily blast of the shofar and the readings of these haftorahs, we learn that our own past may have to be destroyed for us to build again. We may be afraid that we don't know how to prepare for such a total remaking of ourselves or perhaps even that we may prove inadequate to the task.

Using the Wisdom of Our Tradition

That's what this book is all about: drawing upon the wisdom of our tradition, this volume will help you move through a process each day during the month of Elul and through the initial ten days of Tishrei from Rosh Hashanah to Yom Kippur. In addition to a meditation on Psalm 27, which Jewish tradition has selected to help frame our thoughts during this period, we offer other texts to help guide you home. These texts echo themes suggested by Psalm 27 and are presented on intervening days throughout the text. They are culled primarily from two medieval works: *Sha-arei T'shuvah (Gates of Repentance)* by Rabbi Jonah of Gerona and *Hilkhot T'shuvah (Laws of Repentance)* by Moses Maimonides. We also drew from *The Memoirs of Glükel of Hameln,* translated by Marvin Lowenthal and published by Schocken in 1977, and the *T'khine of the Matriarchs*. Because our book is the result of a dialogue between two writers, you will hear two voices clearly in its pages. Kerry took responsibility primarily for the pages devoted to a presentation of Psalm 27, while Rachel prepared the material for the other texts. A variety of related ideas may call out for expression from each selected text. When we want to offer the reader insight into these additional related themes, we use the traditional term *d'var aḥer* (another word/thing) to introduce them.

Alternating with the pages of text and reflection are spaces for your own ideas and reflections. Based on our discussion of a text, we offer an affirmation or meditation, called by Jewish tradition a *kavannah,* in the form of a short statement to prompt your self-reflection. Let each *kavannah* become your daily focus for doing *t'shuvah*. Below each day's *kavannah,* you will find room to write your own thoughts and feelings as you strive to repair your relationships with others and to repair yourself. Write however and whatever you wish.

According to tradition, Moses descended Mount Sinai on Rosh Ḥodesh Elul (the new moon of Elul) only to find that the Israelites had built a golden calf. After he shattered the two stone tablets in his hands, he once again climbed the mountain to receive a second set. He descended for the second time on the tenth of Tishrei, the day we observe Yom Kippur. We are taught that the Israelites spent the forty days during Moses' second mountain sojourn in *t'shuvah* (repentance), readying themselves to receive God's word. Similarly, each day during Elul and the beginning of Tishrei, we are reminded of our many *t'shuvah* tasks by the alarming blast of the shofar, which rouses us from the slumber to which we may have grown accustomed. The shofar blowing escalates to one hundred blasts on Rosh Hashanah, then concludes the final prayers during the Neilah service on Yom Kippur. Rabbi Isaac Horowitz has offered the following interpretation of the shofar blasts: Each series of blasts begins and ends with *t'kiah*, a whole note. *Sh'varim* and *t'ruah* are broken tones and come in between the soundings of *t'kiah*. Horowitz suggests that on Rosh Hashanah, we each begin whole. Along our year's path, however, we become broken through weakness, pain, mistakes, failure, and loss. Yet the end of each year leads to a new Rosh Hashanah—a new chance to become whole once again.

Real Change is Possible

It is never too late to change. There is always hope. As you work, keep these thoughts alive. The great medieval philosopher Moses Maimonides, the Rambam, describes in his *Hilkhot T'shuvah* the three stages of *t'shuvah*: regret, rejection, and resolution. We first feel sorry for what we did (and so we make amends); then when we are confronted with the sin again, we don't repeat it (that's how we know we really have repented); and finally we commit ourselves to a better life through righteous living (that's what fills our days ahead). His system is just as applicable today as it was when he wrote it. As you work through each of these steps, record in your journal how you approached each one. It will make the work a little easier the next time. The ancient rabbis have written: "And *t'shuvah*, *t'fillah*, and *tzedakah* (repentance, prayer, and righteous deeds) avert the evil decree [of death]" (J. Taanit 2:1). Meditating on these three themes, along with reciting *selihot* (penitential prayers), performing *heshbon hanefesh* (introspection), and "begging *m'hila*" (apologizing and making amends)—the other required activities for Elul and Tishrei—form the basis of the discussions in this book and the journal work that accompanies it.

Journal work helps. It forces us to articulate our ideas and feelings, to help move them from thought to deed. When we see ideas written down, they become real and we are able to address them. Journal writing provides us with a record and helps us to create memories as we review our progress. It also helps us to review our successful attempts at making amends, as well as our failures. When we are prepared to learn from our mistakes, we are in a better position to try again.

It also helps to recite *kavannot,* bits of sacred text that have a message of their own. As we repeat them, we are able to hear them and review them in our heads all day. These *kavannot* help us direct our prayers. They speak to us and help us focus our thoughts. They bring us comfort and keep us steady throughout the day. Daily prayer, the recitation of *selihot* (specific penitential prayers), particularly during this time, helps affirm our faith, allowing us to achieve spiritual balance and tranquility.

The religious themes that call to us at this time of year are insistent and powerful. Even more than acting *upon* us, however, these themes call us to action. They call us to write our own *kavannot* and show that we are ready to make the changes necessary to gain us inclusion in the Book of Life. We are asked to affirm our confidence that we can help guide our own destiny.

*L*isten to what the Torah has to say about the future of our own lives. In Genesis, Adam and Eve are banished from the Garden of Eden because of their sin. After they eat the forbidden fruit from the Tree of Knowledge, they are prohibited from eating the fruit from the Tree of Life that would grant them immortality. According to a rabbinic midrash (commentary) that reflects on this narrative, Adam complained to God about his punishment. He feared that all human beings would blame their mortality on Adam's sin. Adam claimed that he would never be able to live with such a stain on his reputation. "As far as wicked people are concerned," argued Adam, "I don't mind if they are condemned to die and know that I am to blame. But what about the good people? I am afraid that the innocent and the righteous will blame me for their deaths!" God replied to Adam, "Don't worry about others. From now on, each individual will be responsible for presenting an accounting of his [or her] life." Each person is required to write his or her own Book of Life. Therefore, the question of life and death, at least for the coming year, will depend upon each of us and our particular way of living. We therefore pray, "Write us in the Book of Life. Accept these *kavannot ha-lev*, 'the intentions of our heart'."

Psalm 27

Adonai is my light and my life.

    Whom shall I fear?

Adonai is the foundation of my life.

    Whom shall I dread?

When evil-doers come upon me to devour me,

    even my adversaries and foes stumble and fall.

If an army should camp against me,

    my heart will not fear.

    Though war should wage up against me

    Even then will I be confident.

One thing I ask of Adonai

    only this do I seek:

    to live in the house of Adonai

    all the days of my life,

    to gaze upon Adonai's beauty

    to frequent God's temple.

For You conceal me in Your pavilion on the day of evil.

    You hide me in the covert of Your tent.

    You lift me up on a rock.

And now my head will be lifted up above my enemies all around me

    And I will offer sacrifices in Your tabernacle with the sound of trumpets.

    I will sing, yes, I will sing praises to Adonai.

*L*isten Adonai when I cry aloud.

  Have mercy on me; answer me.

  [Your instruction,] seek my face, my heart repeats.

  Your face, O God, do I seek.

Hide not your face from me.

  Do not put your servant off in anger. You are my help.

Forsake me not, nor abandon me.

  O God, [You are] the One who delivers me.

For though my father and my mother have forsaken me

  Adonai will lift me up.

Show me Your way, Adonai,

  and lead me on a level path

  because of my ever-watchful foes.

Deliver me not over unto the will of my adversaries

  For false witnesses have risen up against me

  and those who breathe violence.

If I had not believed to look upon the goodness of God,

  [I would no longer be] in the land of the living.

*L*ook to Adonai [for hope]

  be strong and of good courage.

  Look to Adonai [for faith].

ADAPTED FROM THE JPS 1917 AND 1985 TRANSLATIONS—K.M.O.

Elul

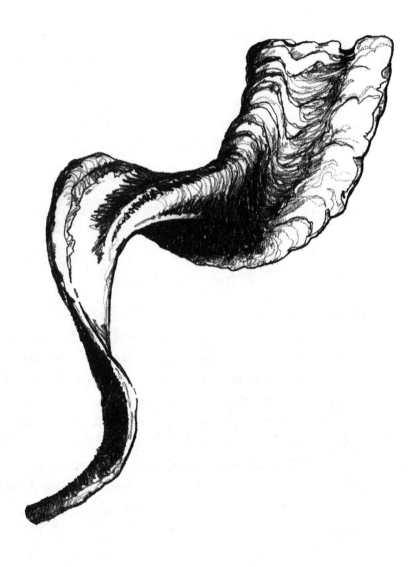

Elul 1

Adonai is my light and my life.
Whom shall I fear?

[Ps. 27:1a]

Forgiveness is difficult whether you are the one who asks for forgiveness or grants it. Even simple words of apology seldom come easily, especially when we are peering into the hidden recesses of our own souls and we know that God is looking in the same place. While it is certainly difficult to say, "I'm sorry," and mean it, such words of remorse are also hard to accept. Frequently, we regard these familiar words as we would the apology of a young child forced by a parent to offer regret to a younger sibling. But we need to recognize that regret is the first step to real change. Without earnest introspection and forgiveness of ourselves and others, we will not change. Only in the reflection of divine light—uncorrupted by the demands of our ego—are we are able to see where we went wrong, what we did to hurt another and how we thereby harmed ourselves.

Our tradition calls this process of self-reflection *ḥeshbon hanefesh*, literally "making an accounting of the soul." It's what the month of Elul is all about. This is a period of preparation, as we anticipate standing naked and humble before God during the High Holy Days period. It takes time to ready ourselves to stand before God. And it takes a lot of work, too. Although these tasks are not easy, Elul does offer us an opportunity to begin again, fully restored to life. Each day, we take stock of our lives, as we consider our actions and interactions over the previous twelve months. Today we begin only with ourselves, unafraid to confront our previous exploits. For in the transformational process of *t'shuvah*, we come to learn that these actions are no longer part of who we are now.

The path of *t'shuvah* is illuminated by divine light.

Elul 2

One must ask oneself: "What have I done?" (Jer. 8:6) What have I become?

[Rabbi Jonah of Gerona, *Gates of Repentance,* First Principle]

*H*ow do we take stock of our actions—and interactions—of the previous year? How do we even begin to confront our misdeeds? We start by letting go of the inescapable fear of discovering what we have done and what we have allowed ourselves to become. Asking these questions of ourselves can be painful. We may prefer to delude ourselves into believing that we can accomplish this task superficially—that we can protect ourselves from what we may find. We certainly have reason to be afraid! But we need to review our deeds of the past year completely, without flinching. We must not let ourselves be seduced into focusing merely on what we have achieved and what we have done well. Elul is a time for confronting the other side of ourselves as well—the darker side that the rabbis call the *yetzer harah*, the "evil inclination."

Acknowledging that we all possess an evil inclination does not exempt us from being responsible for our misdeeds. The *yetzer harah* is not a separate entity over which we have no control. It is part of us. We are accountable for *all* of our deeds. We must not make another our scapegoat. The rabbis teach us to know our evil inclination well, to recognize its ruses, and to learn to defend ourselves against its ill effects. We must learn to redirect its energy toward good and holy ends. We need to acknowledge that we are not perfect, that we have done things that betray the best of what we can become. To conquer our evil inclination, we must reflect on how it has controlled our deeds. The only way that we can repent successfully is by beginning this process.

Hard questions will yield holy answers.

Elul 3

Adonai is the foundation of my life. Whom shall I dread?

[Ps. 27:1b]

*I*t takes a long time for some of us to recognize that God is the foundation of our lives—the foundation of *all* life. Some people never even try to reach that understanding. It might be easier for us if we didn't have to struggle with personal faith, if it came to us with less effort. But that doesn't seem to be the Jewish way. Our tradition teaches us that faith develops—it ebbs and flows. We constantly grapple with issues of faith. As we move through our lives, we are bombarded daily with challenges to that faith. No one is going to come along and provide us with all the answers. Such religious "spoon-feeding" would rob us of the opportunity to achieve spiritual maturity. Remember the story of Jacob's dream? He wrestled with God throughout the night before he was moved to declare, "God was in this place and I never realized it before." Like Jacob, I am prepared to declare: God is with us in this place and every place, no matter how distant divine light seems to be and no matter how profound the darkness. Let us join together to find the light.

This season in the Jewish calendar presents us with many opportunities for spiritual struggling. Each day during the month of Elul and the early days of Tishrei, as we wrestle with our understanding of God, we also confront who and what we are as individuals. Through humble petitional prayers of *seliḥot*, of forgiveness, we ask for divine guidance so that we might muster the strength to change, so that we again might become the person we once aspired to be. So *"Whom should we dread?"* Only the self we used to be—if we allow it to prevent our becoming a new self.

Spiritual growth is possible when we let
go of our past in order to reclaim it.

Elul 4

The Creator has blown into my nostrils a living soul, wisdom of heart and the gift of reason that I might recognize and fear God. . . . After having been created for this purpose and having acted in opposition to it, what is life to me?

[Rabbi Jonah of Gerona, *Gates of Repentance*, First Principle]

*T*he more we become aware of God as our Creator, the more we understand what God's purpose for us is. Then we are able to know how we have fulfilled or frustrated God's plan. In Elul, we are encouraged to take a look at how and what we are doing with the precious living soul God has breathed into us. We come to appreciate that God has given us life; this alone should inspire us to act in accordance with God's will. Moreover, God has given us "wisdom of heart and the gift of reason" so that we might recognize how we have acted in opposition to God's purpose.

*U*sing these gifts of wisdom and reason, we are able to discern between what we have become and what we are striving to become. With this holy gift of recognition, we see which of our actions were holy and helped to fulfill God's plan, and which were unholy. We are also able to differentiate the three parties against whom we have sinned this year: God, others, and ourselves. Consulting our heart of wisdom we know, as Maimonides discovered centuries ago, that different kinds of sin require different kinds of confession. For our sins against God, or God's plan, we must seek divine forgiveness. For our sins against others, we must acknowledge our wrongdoings and ask forgiveness from those whom we have wronged. And for our sins against ourselves, we must accept that we have damaged our own lives. Although it is dizzying to try to turn simultaneously in three directions at once, we understand that the more purposefully we turn, the more our lives will have purpose.

By doing *t'shuvah*, we can look in three directions at once: to God, to self, and to others.

Elul 5

When evil-doers come upon me to devour me,
even my adversaries and foes stumble and fall.

[Ps. 27:2]

Sometimes we think, "*T'shuvah* can't work if I am the only one doing it. It's lonely work. And anyhow, how can I ever let my guard down? Can I really change when there are those who want to do me harm? Whether they are competitors in business or colleagues at work or school just striving to get ahead, they want to see me stumble and fall. Perhaps they are unwilling to admit it, but they'll be first in line to take my place." We might think that's how the world is supposed to work, but it need not be.

T'shuvah provides us with a prism through which to view the world. By working on ourselves rather than attempting to change others, we may find that those whom we thought were enemies are in fact people just like ourselves. We can change them only by changing ourselves. Those who think otherwise eventually will stumble and fall as they race to get ahead at our expense.

Each of us has the potential to change, no matter how far we have strayed from the path of the good life. Waiting for others to change first, however, won't help us change. The Baal Shem Tov said, "Sinners are mirrors. When we see faults in them we should realize that they only reflect the evil in ourselves." *T'shuvah* is possible only through changing ourselves. These days of Elul provide us with that opportunity to change. We can do it, because God will help us. We will not stumble or fall, because God is at our side.

The only place to walk is in God's presence.

Elul 6

> **"There is not a righteous person on earth who does [only] good and does not sin" (Eccles. 7:20). However, [the righteous] subdue their evil inclination a hundred times. If they have succumbed to a sin once, they do not repeat it, to prevent becoming loathsome in their own eyes; and [so] they repent.**
>
> [Rabbi Jonah of Gerona, *Gates of Repentance*, The First Gate, p. 9]

We all have sinned. There is not a single one among us who has not. Even when we are "righteous," we still sin. What ultimately matters is not *whether* we sin, but how we respond to the reality of sinning. When we have learned this Torah about life and can begin to admit that we sometimes sin, that we sometimes fail, then we can begin to figure out how to respond, how to stand erect again. It helps that we know that God is walking at our side and that we are not alone. Rabbi Jonah teaches us that repentance is motivated also by our own desire not to become "loathsome" in our own eyes. Although we may be able to rid ourselves of guilt over a *specific* act—whether by trying to "make up for it" or by making a "guilt offering" like the ancients—we still carry guilt. This is because when we consider *all* of our actions, we feel more than guilty: we become "loathsome" in our own eyes. The key is to allow this negative energy to move us to do *t'shuvah*. Regarded this way, self-loathing is not a hurdle, but a motivating force. The stronger it is, the more powerfully we are propelled toward *t'shuvah*.

Think for a moment about a sinful act or thought from the past year that you repeated at least once, and for which you now "loathe" yourself. Now imagine in your mind the person you are striving to become. By doing *t'shuvah*, you can transform yourself from the person you loathe into the person you hope to become. Through *t'shuvah* you can recreate yourself.

By doing *t'shuvah*, you participate in the act of *recreation*.

Elul 7

If an army should camp against me,
my heart will not fear.
Though war should wage up against me
Even then will I be confident.

[Ps. 27:3]

These words demonstrate a powerful faith. I think to myself, "Can my faith ever be *that* strong?" That's why we repeat the psalmist's words in our heart: to give us strength and confidence in our faith when we feel it wavering. Of course, there are times when our faith in God and ourselves is resolute, when nothing can challenge it. We get up each day, feeling secure in the knowledge that our soul has been returned to us—and in much better shape than it was the night before. On most days, however, we struggle, looking for evidence of God's work in our lives. And that's when we realize that we may be looking in the wrong places. God's presence is found in the rhythm of everyday living. That's the miracle.

But we constantly have to do things to renew our own faith. God can't do that for us. We must perform spiritual exercise to retain and build our spiritual strength. It does not come on its own. That's one of the reasons our people have been reciting psalms for generations. The rabbis understood the spiritual power of psalms. In addition to enriching the liturgy with them, they assigned one to each day of the week and to special seasons of the year (like Psalm 27 during this season of repentance). Rabbi Eugene Borowitz says that psalms give us the vehicle to say things that we thought we were incapable of saying or simply are unable to say. As you begin to work things out in your life and make amends with people you have harmed, bring your burdens to God. You'll be surprised at what you are able to say.

Miracles can be found only when we are ready to look for them.

Elul 8

How does one acknowledge sin? One says: I implore You God. . . . Behold, I regret [what I did] and am embarrassed by my deeds. I promise never to repeat this act again.

[Moses Maimonides, *Laws of Repentance* 1:1]

*E*mbarrassment does not have to stand in the way of our *t'shuvah*; instead, it can move us further toward *t'shuvah*. Embarrassment, like self-loathing, is not encouraged by contemporary psychology. The rabbis, however, have a different sense of what moves us to change. When we feel embarrassed before God about what we have done—and we regret having done it—we feel ourselves commanded to change, to create ourselves anew. Our sense of self, as well the image of ourselves that we imagine God sees, demands that we do *t'shuvah*. We remember that we do not have to remain fixed in a stagnant version of self. Each of us has the opportunity to emerge from our humiliation over what we did to become our essential self, unashamed of our past behavior, and recreated in our new behavior.

Becoming someone and something else, however, means first confronting who we are. It means confessing aloud to God, and thereby to ourselves, each action we regret and about which we are embarrassed, and then promising to act differently next time. By making promises about the future, we declare that we have faith in our ability to do things differently, if given the chance. We must review those acts we regret and tell God and ourselves how we will try to handle each situation differently next time. By giving us another year, God is giving us another chance. What we make of this opportunity, what we make of ourselves in the year to come, depends on our doing *t'shuvah* now.

Embarrassment and regret pave the road to change.

Elul 9

*One thing I ask of Adonai
only this do I seek:
to live in the house of Adonai
all the days of my life,
to gaze upon Adonai's beauty,
to frequent God's temple.*

[Ps. 27:4]

*H*ow wonderful it would be just to remain in God's presence all day, every day, as the psalmist says, "to live in the house of Adonai all the days of my life." As a matter of fact, we already do. We just don't always realize it. When the Torah was given at Sinai, there was complete silence instead of an anticipated blast of noise. Six hundred thousand people stood at the foot of the mountain in the wilderness of the desert, and no one talked, nothing moved. We didn't even hear the flapping of birds winging their way across the sky. There was total silence unmarred by noise of any kind. Only in this way could everyone hear the divine message. God hasn't stopped speaking to us since that day at Sinai, but there is so much noise in the world that we are prevented from hearing God's voice.

*S*o what can we do? We need to get rid of the many noises that distract us. Our world is too full of them. We need to listen to and then still the inner voice tugging at our gut, reminding us that we have done something we should not have done. Even if what we did months ago seemed inconsequential at the time, the time now has come to ask for forgiveness—what our tradition calls begging m'hila—from those we love. If we don't, that inner voice will get so loud that we may never be able to hear God's voice. Seek out those whom you have wronged and then listen carefully. What you hear may astonish you.

The voice from Sinai is heard in silence.

Elul 10

Who has achieved complete t'shuvah? A person who confronts the same situation in which he [or she] sinned and abstains, although that person has the potential to commit the sin again.

[Moses Maimonides, *Laws of Repentance* 2:1]

Becoming someone else means reimagining who we are. T'shuvah means turning from who we were into someone different, someone who behaves differently. It means envisioning ourselves returning to an earlier situation but making another choice this time, doing it differently. The rabbis forbid us to offer prayers that ask to alter what has already occurred in the past. Rather, they teach us that God demands *t'shuvah*. We pray that our future actions and their consequences will be different.

It's difficult to imagine ourselves doing differently everything we regret about the past year. So let's take a single past event and envision ourselves responding differently this time. Remember the moments just before you acted. Try to remember who you were and what you were thinking. Did you carefully consider what you were doing? Did you weigh the consequences? Did you have any idea then how ashamed you would be now?

Think to yourself and pray, "God, I am trying to remember exactly what I was thinking then. I do not know how I could have behaved that way. Had I the sense of Your presence and of who I want to be in Your eyes and in my own, I might have acted differently." When we imagine ourselves in that same situation in the future, we know that we will respond differently because of our *t'shuvah*. For that act, at least, our *t'shuvah* is complete.

Complete acts of *t'shuvah* help complete the self.

Elul 11

For You conceal me in Your pavilion on the day of evil.
You hide me in the covert of Your tent.
You lift me up on a rock.

[Ps. 27:5]

Feeling angry about what we have done, we often fear that there is nothing we can do to change what already has occurred. Our children have grown older. The people we have wronged have moved away, forgotten what happened, or even passed from this earth. But we still feel that we need to do something to restore order to our lives. Rabbi Lawrence Kushner teaches that past events are not fixed; rather, he says that they—and our relationship to them—can change. Only the unknown future is static. Although this notion seems the opposite of what we might expect, we can make sense of it when we recognize that we can change the past through how we understand it. Joseph, who lived thousands of years ago, came to understand this religious truth. He finally realized that neither he nor his brothers were in control of his descent into Egypt. Because of Joseph's new understanding, the "evil" action of Joseph's brothers—throwing him into the pit and selling him into slavery—took on another dimension. Had Joseph not arrived in Egypt, he would not have been able to provide food for his family during the years of famine. Sometimes all it takes is a different perspective to change events in the past.

The rabbis say that acts of *tzedakah* and gifts of kindness, when accompanied by *t'shuvah* and *t'fillah*, actually can change the harsh decree of Yom Kippur. For some, this notion may be only a metaphor. For others, a life of *tzedakah* is an actual ideal toward which to strive. No matter which perspective you take, understand the power of *tzedakah* to encourage individual change. That's the peculiar thing about *tzedakah*: as we give to others, we are able to reclaim ourselves. As you give *tzedakah*, remember that the life you save may be your own.

The present contains the potential to change the past.

Elul 12

> [The sin offering] atones for all the transgressions in the Torah . . . those violated intentionally and those transgressed inadvertently; those which the transgressor becomes conscious of and those which he [or she] is not conscious of. . . . But this only applies if one repents.
>
> [Moses Maimonides, *Laws of Repentance* 1:2]

*W*hat is my "sin offering" today? What can I possibly give or do or say to atone for what I have done? My sin offering is this very process of t'shuvah, looking inward and then removing all the "garbage," getting rid of it, resolving that next year I will not recreate the refuse. Asking forgiveness for sins we committed inadvertently comes fairly easily—we expect to be forgiven automatically. Facing the things we did intentionally is harder, however, because these actions force us to recognize how much we need to change. Because we did them consciously, we are afraid that they may be embedded deep within us. That's why we are not always confident we can turn from them fully. Because we are aware of them, however, we can pay more attention to these tendencies and resolve to watch ourselves vigilantly, lest we give in to them again.

But how can we do t'shuvah for things of which we are not conscious? What can be our sin offering for an unknown sin? How can we offer something appropriate to atone for our acts? We know we can't remember everything that happened in the previous year. We know we have hurt others and sinned against God and ourselves without knowing it. We surely don't want to invent extra sins, but we must leave room in our t'shuvah process to atone for unknown and unnameable sins. Deep beneath our consciousness lies more "toxic waste."

Once we clean up the environment of our souls, we can breathe freely.

And now my head will be lifted up above my enemies all around me
And I will offer sacrifices in Your tabernacle with the sound of trumpets.
I will sing, yes, I will sing praises to Adonai.
[Ps. 27:6]

Spiritual moments in life don't always come when we want them, expect them or even need them. In my own journey, I have learned that they can be encouraged but never forced. Lots of things help make these moments possible. Scrubbing the soul clean helps. So do prayer and introspection, especially during this time of year. Don't forget *tzedakah* either. Often these spiritual moments last only for a brief flash in time. We momentarily feel lifted on angels' wings. In response, our heart overflows with song. Then we fall silent, listening for our inner voice to continue its song.

Maybe this is all the motivation we need to do what we have avoided for years. Routine seems to steal our ideals from us. Only when we feel as though we have made every effort to change do we realize that still more work remains to be done. Humbled by the task of doing *t'shuvah*, we realize that it's finally time to realign the course of our life, no matter how daunting change seems. Nothing less will do. As we gather the strength necessary for the task ahead, we reach deep inside and remind ourselves, "And now my head will be lifted up above my enemies all around me. . . ."

D'var *aḥer:* Get ready for Rosh Hashanah by getting yourself ready for a *new* year. Everything falls into place when you make room for God. Remember what Menaḥem Mendl of Kotzk said in response to the question: Where is God? The Kotzker replied, "Wherever we let God in."

Spiritual moments contain eternity.

Elul 14

At present . . . there is no altar of atonement;
there remains nothing else aside from t'shuvah.

[Moses Maimonides, *Laws of Repentance* 1:3]

Once we placed our sacrifices on an altar. We offered these sacrifices—individually and collectively—in a complex priestly ritual, seeking atonement. The sacrificial ceremony became our dialogue with God: a concrete activity, a tangible process, by which a person could fulfill the demands of t'shuvah. Today, however, the altar and the Temple are gone, and we are left adrift, with prayer alone as our spiritual offering to mediate between God and us. We cannot make a regular pilgrimage to Jerusalem and offer up a goat or a dove, believing that we will be expiated for our transgressions. We are left only with ourselves, our prayers, and the offerings of our souls.

In place of the altar stands our being. What we offer up to God during these few weeks of Elul are pieces of what we have become: we offer up words of prayer that express gratitude for the ways in which we have thrived and regret for the ways in which we have fallen short. But we can't see any "pleasing smoke," no *reah niḥoah*, such as that which was visible to the ancient Israelites standing around the altar. We see nothing wafting up toward God to arouse divine compassion and forgiveness. Searching through the moral casualties of the past year, however, we also find what has been "slaughtered," and as we mentally offer it up and let it go, we feel it let us go, too. Lifting the heaviness of old anger is a way of letting go of the stuff we have been shlepping around with us. The *reah niḥoah* that emerges from these offerings, the letting go of what keeps us stuck, cannot be seen or smelled, yet it too arouses and allows for forgiveness.

When we offer up sacrifices, we let go of our inner selves.

Elul 15

Listen Adonai when I cry aloud.
Have mercy on me; answer me.

[Ps. 27:7]

Listen. Please God, listen to me. It's all that I ask. I know I may not always deserve it. But I come before You, having cleansed the broken pieces of my soul. I struggle daily to repair what I have done wrong, to redirect the course my life has taken over these past months. The effort consumes me. It's all that I can think about, all that occupies my waking hours. And just when my strength seems depleted, I feel renewed through the process of repentance. I long to be restored to wholeness. I turn to You, knowing that I can achieve it only through my relationship with You.

When we pray, we want God to respond. Rabbi Naḥman of Bratzlav, the Bratzlaver Rebbe, taught us about the silent scream, the kind that escapes from deep within our soul—erupting when we least expect it, without making a sound. "Help me!" we scream silently. Although we are working hard to prepare ourselves for the New Year, t'shuvah doesn't always seem to work precisely the way we planned. Something gets in our way, blocking our intention to change, no matter how hard we work. But that's the nature of the human path to change: winding and circuitous with roadblocks everywhere. Often we get in our own way. It is time for us to get out of our way and start on God's way.

We want God to hear us, whatever the nature of our prayer. We feel that we are doing our share of the work. Now we ask God to do what God is supposed to do—to help heal us. We pray that when Yom Kippur arrives, we will be able to stand erect before God, whole once again.

Prayer is part of an ongoing dialogue with the Divine.

Elul 16

There are sins that can be atoned for immediately and other sins which can only be atoned for over the course of time.

[Moses Maimonides, *Laws of Repentance* 1:4]

T'shuvah is not a single act or a single moment of personal transformation. Rather, it is a lengthy process, a daily struggle that our tradition emphasizes during this month and a half of the Jewish calendar. This focus on our own transformation, on repentance and renewal during Elul and Tishrei, however, is framed by the remainder of the Jewish calendar, which demands daily t'shuvah. We must recognize that despite the intense pressure on us during this time of year, some of the t'shuvah we need to do cannot happen just yet. Some of what we must repent for, ask forgiveness for, and a great deal of what we want to become must be left for the coming year.

Rabbi Abraham Isaac Kook, like Maimonides, taught that t'shuvah can be sudden or gradual. Sometimes repentance is instantaneous, forgivenesss is immediate, and change is felt at the moment. But there is also a slower, more gradual repentance. In this case, the movement toward regret and forgiveness involves tiny steps. Each small attempt to transform ourselves is nearly imperceptible. "Sudden repentance," according to Rabbi Kook's categories, "derives from a spiritual flash entering the soul . . . immediately the person experiences inwardly a complete change for good." Gradual repentance, on the other hand, results from a feeling inside that tells us we must go forward and improve our ways. T'shuvah, both sudden and gradual, is open to us when we are open to it.

It takes a lifetime to complete the process of *t'shuvah*.

Elul 17

*[Your instruction,] seek my face, my heart repeats.
Your face, O God, do I seek.*

[Ps. 27:8]

*W*hat is it about the High Holy Days that draws us into the synagogue? Even those of us who can't find our way during the year seek out the synagogue at this time. Perhaps the High Holy Days are designed especially for those who can't find their way, who get lost somewhere between one Yom Kippur and the next. Of course, some will scoff, claiming that the synagogue is no place for once-a-year Jews. Don't listen to them. Remember what the rabbis have taught us: the gates of prayer may be open only at certain times, but the gates of repentance are always open to us.

Sometimes, we have to reach deep inside ourselves to discover our path to repentance. It's hard work; that's probably why we shy away from it. But God beckons us, for God remembers all—even what we have forgotten. Throughout our lives, as we go through the many doors of our experience, we take directions we never considered as children. As we grow older, the doors seem to close tightly behind us. This period of preparing for Elul is all about forcing open those doors and going back through them to rediscover our essential selves, the ones that God is seeking. The medieval poet Judah Halevi said, "When I go forth looking for You, I find You seeking me." In the process of looking for God, we also find ourselves.

The gates of repentance are always open.

Elul 18

There are many levels of repentance through which one draws near to the Holy Blessed One. And although there is forgiveness in relation to each kind of repentance, the soul does not become completely purified . . . unless one purifies one's heart and properly conditions one's spirit.

[Rabbi Jonah of Gerona, *Gates of Repentance,* The First Gate]

The soul and the spirit, two aspects of our personality that often seem elusive, now must be brought to the surface so that our t'shuvah will last beyond this particular moment or this particular month. We seek to become intimate with our souls and our spirits, to give voice to our inner selves, so we can draw near to God. Feeling close to God will ease our struggle for repentance and personal repair. Yet so many things get in our way, especially our unfamiliarity with our spiritual selves. If we fail to "purify" this deeper level within us, our t'shuvah will remain only a surface change. If we reach deep inside, however, and touch that part of us too often suffocated underneath the refuse of daily life, our t'shuvah will take root at the core of who we are. Only in this way can we be transformed. Only through this kind of reaching, digging, knowing, and changing can we prevent ourselves from revisiting the ugliness and sins of the past.

As we continue our journey, we gradually will become accustomed to the loneliness that so often accompanies this kind of deep self-exploration. As we become familiar with the struggle of self, spirit, and soul—and our emerging closeness with God—the gates will open for our t'shuvah. Seek the courage to weather the changes. God's presence eases our pain and decreases our loneliness; then we can feel God's presence even more.

Repentance is an act of belief in the future.

Elul 19

Hide not your face from me.
  Do not put your servant off in anger. You are
  my help.
Forsake me not, nor abandon me.
  O God, [You are] the One who delivers me.
  [Ps. 27:9]

Some believe that searching for God is like playing hide-and-seek. If this is so, why might God be hiding from us? What have we done to distance God's presence from us? Have we stolen? Committed murder? No, most of us are not guilty of such terrible crimes. Instead, it's the little transgressions—those so woven into the fabric of our lives that we often fail to recognize them—that have concealed God from us. These missteps that start out small accumulate over time to become much larger than we ever thought possible.

Consider the life you lead and your relationships with others. How do you treat those you encounter on the street and those with whom you work? What about those whom you love? Have your actions threatened the sacred trust of those relationships? The High Holy Days—and our preparation for them—provide us with the chance to change. When we do, we'll find that God won't be hiding anymore. As we seek God, we can then say, "O God, [You *are*] the One who delivers me. Forsake me not, nor abandon me." Rabbi Abraham Joshua Heschel taught that the whole earth is full of ways to inquire of You. Even if you have given up seeking God, God still seeks you.

When we change the direction of our life, we will
find that God has been there waiting for us.

Elul 20

What constitutes t'shuvah? *That sinners should abandon [their] sins and remove them from [their] thoughts, resolving in [their] hearts never to commit them again. . . . One must verbally confess and state these matters which have been resolved in one's heart.*

[Moses Maimonides, *Laws of Repentance* 2:2]

The rabbis constructed many different systems of repentance, all of which operate on the principle that *t'shuvah* occurs in stages, each new stage depending on the one before. The process is a stairway ascending toward Heaven. The goal is to draw near to God. We must tread each step of the stairway—at least briefly—to "get there." Even at the first step, however, we begin to change. We can decide to quit a bad habit "cold turkey"—to stop a destructive behavior and wipe it from our minds, resolving never to do it again. The rabbis teach that we must not only stop a certain behavior but must also speak about our *t'shuvah,* describing how the behavior is wrong and how we have resolved to change in our hearts.

With all our modern knowledge of psychology, we may be skeptical that sudden change through *t'shuvah* is possible. We know that those recovering from addictive behaviors—smoking, drinking, taking drugs, overeating, compulsive sexual behavior—rarely succeed in suddenly changing their behavior. We recognize that to change such powerfully motivated and ingrained habits we must make a step-by-step climb toward a better self. But still we must, despite our ugly behaviors and shame about ourselves, face that first step. We may feel unsteady. We may be thrown off balance as we leave our familiar selves, but we need to reach that next level, that next step. Only there can we hope for a better future, to get closer to God.

Lasting change comes in stages.

Elul 21

For though my father and my mother have forsaken me
Adonai will lift me up.

[Ps. 27:10]

*W*hy would the psalmist have suggested that our parents have forsaken us? For some of us, it is unfortunately true, and we must find the inner strength to let go of that pain. Most of us, however, simply have to come to understand that eventually we all have to stand on our own, fully accountable for who we are and what we have become. Our parents are no longer responsible—they can't protect us as they may have when we were children. If our parents continue to sustain us in adulthood, we become "adult children."

The month of Elul is all about growing up and letting go of childhood—and the many childish relationships we may have carried into our adult lives. We need to release all the bitterness of family rivalries that gripped us while we still lived under our parents' roofs—such bitterness led Cain to kill his brother. Even worse than our urge to strike out at those we love is this internal poison that is killing us—and those around us—a little at a time. Keep in mind the teaching of Rabbi Yitzḥak, who wrote, "One's impulse renews itself to evil everyday. It grows in strength each day and seeks to slay you" (B. Sukkah 52b).

D'var aḥer: Don't wait to repair the path. Do it now. It will help pave your way home.

As we become adults, we encounter our parents with new understanding.

Elul 22

Among the ways to repent for the one turning is...to change his name, as if to say, I am a different person and not the same one who sinned.

[Moses Maimonides, *Laws of Repentance* 2:4]

*P*aradoxically, the achievement of *t'shuvah* involves self-acceptance along with radical change of the self. Maimonides expresses this paradox by pointing to the powerful act of changing one's name as if to say, "I am a different person." The hope that we can change and become different energizes us. Our desire to move away from the old, to embrace a new self, propels us through the gates of repentance that now stand open before us. Knowing that the gates will close at the end of the Yom Kippur Neilah service motivates us to hurry forward with our *t'shuvah*.

Name changes occur numerous times in the Bible, where they often symbolize a new relationship between the individual and God. Abram becomes Abraham. Sarai becomes Sarah. Jacob becomes Israel. Taking on a new name was part of a covenant-making between the individual and the Holy One. One who sins cuts him- or herself off in some way from God, but one who repents returns to God, rededicating him- or herself to the relationship. Joseph Soloveitchik taught that such renewal brings an individual back within the framework of the complete agreement that rests on the dual connection: between God and the people of Israel and between God and the individual in the community of Israel. Newly named, we return to God, announcing anew our desire to be in a sacred relationship. Like Jacob, however, we first must wrestle with unidentified angels, and with those parts of ourselves manifest only in the midst of darkness.

To get to the light, we have to find our way through the darkness.

Elul 23

*Show me Your way, Adonai,
and lead me on a level path
because of my ever-watchful foes.*

[Ps. 27:11]

*T*here is no other way to say it: If we want to restore our lives to order, we have to turn to God. We can't rely only on ourselves any longer. We see the dead ends toward which that approach has taken us. Although *t'shuvah* may require only a slight turning, that's all it takes to point us in a completely different direction.

*T*he path of repentance is neither short nor direct. We should not be fooled into thinking otherwise. These days of Elul will just get us started on our way. Once we have begun our spiritual journey, however, it doesn't matter how long it takes—or where it takes us—because we'll know that we are going in the right direction.

*R*abbi Yose ben Halafta was once asked what God had been doing since the creation of the world. His response: "Making ladders for people to descend and ascend" (Leviticus Rabbah 8:1). We've all been on those ladders going in both directions: climbing, teetering, falling. Maybe the sages were right when they claimed that our people could not have entered Canaan had they not been first enslaved in Egypt. Only when we were ready for freedom could we make our way through the desert toward the Promised Land.

*W*hat did we learn in the desert? That our enemies may want us to stumble and fall, but God wants us to right ourselves and continue.

Whenever we get lost in the desert, God helps us find our way.

Elul 24

The kernel of Torah is "You shall love your neighbor as yourself." But in our day we seldom find it so, and few are they who love their fellowmen [and women] with all their heart. On the contrary, if a person can contrive to ruin one's neighbor, nothing pleases him more.

[*The Memoirs of Glükel of Hameln,* Trans. Marvin Lowenthal]

As we become aware through doing t'shuvah of the parts of ourselves we must shed, we can begin to admit how we may have hurt others. We can acknowledge that we sometimes have forgotten the counsel that "you should love your neighbor as yourself." Reviewing our behavior during of the past year, we realize that we often have released at others the anger we should have directed at ourselves. And yet we also must learn to forgive ourselves. How else can we learn to love our neighbors as ourselves?

We cannot really love others until we love ourselves. Loving ourselves, however, as we take stock of all the wrong we have done and realize all the t'shuvah we have yet to do, becomes increasingly difficult. We should be gentle with ourselves as we engage in the process of change. By forgiving ourselves and by embracing who we are becoming through the process of t'shuvah we gradually come to love ourselves more. Then we are able to love others.

Rabbi Levi Yitzhak of Berditchev taught that our ability to love others is indicative of our ability to love God. "Whether a person really loves God," the Berditchever said, "can be determined by the love that person shares with others."

Love of others is possible only through love of self.

Elul 25

Deliver me not over unto the will of my adversaries
> *For false witnesses have risen up against me and those who breathe violence.*

[Ps. 27:12]

Before he offered his evening prayers, Rabbi Isaac Luria, the great medieval kabbalist, would begin: "I hereby forgive all who hurt me this day." Ridding himself of everything that might weigh him down during prayer—"taking his heart in his hands," as our tradition puts it—he was able to lift himself heavenward. Although we may find it difficult to follow Luria's example, we can try each time we enter the synagogue to leave our baggage outside the sanctuary door.

It's easy to hide behind the illusion that we are always righteous—to believe that everyone else is out to get us and anxious to see us fail. These thoughts spring from our own self-doubt, however, and become part of our inner core, threatening to destroy us. Before we take apart the world around us, piece by piece, we need to look in the mirror. We may find there the adversary we fear.

Try the method of Rabbi Levi Yitzhak of Berditchev. Each night before going to bed, he would make a list of all he had done wrong that day. Reciting it over and over, he would be overcome with regret and remorse, so much so that he would begin to cry. Only after his tears had wiped the paper clean of ink was he able to face the night and the day that followed. Levi Yitzhak teaches us that this season of inner searching is not about seeking perfection. Rather, it is simply about acknowledging our human fragility and imperfection.

Faith comes on the road to forgiveness.

[Torah] is like a rope which the great and gracious God has thrown to us as we drown in the stormy sea of life, that we may seize hold of it and be saved.

[*The Memoirs of Glükel of Hameln,* Trans. Marvin Lowethal]

Getting to know the Torah better during this month of Elul will help us get to know God a bit better. What will help us in our struggle is reaching for a few words of Torah each day by reading the Psalms, studying the High Holy Days prayer book, or reading the pages of this book. We need not go through the process of *t'shuvah* alone. Words of Torah, which connect us to God, can provide good company. The ancient sages, as well as the teachers of our day, advise us to reach out for Torah daily. Rabbi Jacob Moses Ḥarlap writes that daily study helps us to draw near to God and to replenish our sensitivity to the holy. According to Rabbi Abraham Isaac Kook, studying Torah draws us near to our true perfection, which is the purpose of life.

Striving toward our own perfection is a first stage in striving toward perfecting the world. Studying the Torah and doing *t'shuvah* teaches us that by perfecting ourselves we become God's partners in perfecting the world. Speaking the words of Torah and prayer, hearing the words of our own hearts, and yearning silently for the transcendent are our ways of reaching for God's light. They allow us to perceive ourselves and to know God in a light that we otherwise might not see.

Set for yourself a time each day or each week to study the Torah's sacred words.

Through Torah, God will help us see ourselves.

Elul 27

If I had not believed I would look upon the goodness of God,
[I would no longer be] in the land of the living.

[Ps. 27:13]

My faith keeps me alive, for I believe in God's power to heal and invigorate. As the prophet Jeremiah taught, ". . . the word [of God] is like a raging fire in my heart, shut up in my bones. I try to rein it in, but I cannot" (Jeremiah 20:9). Even though we may be apprehensive about echoing aloud the prophet's powerful sentiments, we must be willing to do so. For we have been witnesses to God's work in the world. Furthermore, because all of us respond differently to God, the Torah was revealed to us in different languages, so that we all could hear its voice and convey its message in our own words.

Menaḥem Mendl of Kotzk taught that the "only whole heart is a broken one." A similar insight is found in the teaching of another rebbe who explained that he was able to understand others' shortcomings only because he saw them in himself. Once when a disciple came to him and the rebbe found that he could not reach into the depth of this disciple's sins, the rebbe knew that he would have to look more deeply into his own failings. This is a great *t'shuvah* lesson to learn: we should not look for our own shortcomings in others. We must find them first in ourselves. We won't have to go looking far. Regardless of who we are or how successful we have become, we are all in need of repair. We may not always understand how God's plan for us works in our life, but we can feel God's presence making its will known. Regardless of where we try to go, God always helps us find the way there.

Healing begins when we acknowledge that we are broken.

Elul 28

Every day, every hour, and every moment of my life I have sinned, nearly all manner of sins. God grant that I may find the means and occasion for repentance. . . . But, alas, . . . the ways of the world, have kept me far from that state.

[*The Memoirs of Glükel of Hameln,* Trans. Marvin Lowethal]

The process of *t'shuvah* could be a full time job. But we have so many other responsibilities, that we have little time to ask others for forgiveness. We need to remind ourselves that even a small amount of time devoted to *t'shuvah* can change our lives and the lives of others. Rabbi Abraham Isaac Kook taught that "a little study bears fruit in all of one's deeds and learning, just as the brain, although small in size, imprints the human form in human beings."

*F*ulfilling all our responsibilities to our families, our workplaces, and our communities demands so much of us that we may wonder how we can squeeze in this "extra" task of *t'shuvah*. What we may forget is that fulfilling these responsibilities provides us with constant opportunities for repentance. Slightly changing the tone we use with a coworker, a parent, a child, or a sibling will open for us a gate that leads to even greater change. We need to remind ourselves that each person we encounter is created *b'tzelem Elohim*—in the image of God. Therefore, being more gentle, more honest, more loving, and more forgiving toward another will bring us closer not only to that person but also to God. Striving to be more God-like in the world is not something that has to be forced into our schedules. Rather, God demands that we schedule everything else around this essential task.

Because the world is a different place each moment
I am alive, there is unlimited potential for change.

Elul 29

Look to Adonai [for hope]
be strong and of good courage.
Look to Adonai [for faith].

[Ps. 27:14]

Sometimes we get depressed, especially after nearly a month of piercing self-reflection and personal scrutiny. Ahead of us still lies the difficult task of begging m'hila—asking forgiveness from those whom we have wronged. How deflated we now feel after regarding ourselves for so many years as stable adults. Added to all the other pressures we feel in our daily lives, such gut-wrenching work threatens to overwhelm us. It's tough enough just making it through each day, and our lives become even more difficult when we are surrounded by illness and the deaths of those we love. But we need not give up. "Look to Adonai [for hope]." We need not despair. "Be strong and of good courage." Instead we should focus our sights on that fiery mountaintop in the desert of Sinai, where God once made a covenant with the Jewish people that is renewed daily. Even though we recall that covenant formally during the late spring festival of Shavuot, we can celebrate that relationship informally each day through our spiritual practice.

The summer is over. We near the end of a tumultuous year. As we grow older, each year seems increasingly shorter and sterner. We eagerly look forward to embracing Rosh Hashanah—now just around the corner—even though its liturgy sounds a clarion call for judgment. We finally have realized that the daily shofar blasts we have heard during this month of Elul are a warning to us: redirect your energies and establish new priorities for living, or remain lost. Take your compass in hand. "Look to Adonai [for faith]." If we redirect ourselves toward God, we will always be going in the right direction.

At the end of the year, we find a new beginning.

At the Close of Elul

This is the last moment; for I know how much time I have let slip away without turning in repentance.

[*T'khine of the Matriarchs for the Shofar*]

*A*s Elul comes to an end, we realize that we have just begun our work of *t'shuvah*. We look back with regret at the time we have "wasted" without turning in repentance. Although the opportunities were many and they presented themselves to us daily, we probably were unable or perhaps unwilling to take advantage of them. Time is slipping away; soon it will be Rosh Hashanah. Though we may panic, we also take heart as we acknowledge the exciting potential for the coming year. The blasts of the shofar startle us with their wake-up call, proclaiming that it is never too late to turn in repentance.

Before the new moon ushers in the month of Tishrei, a storm strikes our soul, stirring panic within us. We have so many things to say to others and ourselves! In the calm before and after this storm, we are unable to break open our hearts, but each year, the storm roiling in our souls can free us to speak.

Make a new beginning. Write a letter to someone you know you have hurt in the last year. Resolve to abandon one bad habit. Study at least one line of Torah. Learn one new prayer. Make a plan to improve one way you relate to others. God will take note of our repentance, study, prayer, and loving acts, and will join us in our efforts to perfect this precious world. When we affirm anew our covenant with God, we are affirmed.

The shofar calls us to remember the future.

Tishrei: The Ten Days of Awe

Tishrei 1—Rosh Hashanah

Go your way, eat rich foods and drink sweet beverages; send portions to the one who has nothing prepared, for this day is holy to Adonai. Do not be sad, for joy is in Adonai, your refuge.

[Neh. 8:10]

With these words, Nehemiah tempered the harsh warning of Ezra, who retaught the law to the Jews exiled in Babylonia. The name Nehemiah resonates with the Hebrew word for comfort and consolation, *neḥemta*. Like the Jewish people in Babylonia, many of us today feel exiled from God's presence by our misdeeds and unfulfilled obligations. We dread the coming judgment. As the prophet Amos declared, "Shall the horn [the shofar] be blown in the city and the people not tremble?" (Amos 3:6). Even as we put on our finery for synagogue and celebrate Rosh Hashanah like a gala affair, we know the truth. During these next ten days, our fates will be decided. According to tradition, the thoroughly wicked and the thoroughly righteous already have been judged. These awesome ten days are meant for us, the "middle-of-the-road" sinners, giving us a last chance to make a life or death difference in the world—to affect the decision on our own life or death.

It's the beginning of a new year—time to make a new start. Let us not be discouraged by the many things we still must do to put our lives back in order. As we continue our journey toward wholeness and healing, we need to remember to forgive ourselves along the way. How fervently we hope that, when we sit down for dinner and taste the apple dipped in honey, this traditional prayer will reflect the stirrings of our heart: "May it be Your will, our God and God of our ancestors to renew us for a good, sweet year."

T'shuvah sweetens our journey toward wholeness.

Tishrei 2—Rosh Hashanah

The great shofar is sounded and a still small voice is heard.

[Maḥzor]

*W*hose voice do we hear beckoning us to change? Is the shofar blast the sound of our own soul, the voice of our heart that we have sought to silence for so many years? Or is it the voice of angels whom God has sent to remind us that we already know what we have to do? Many teachers have suggested meanings for each sounding of the shofar. The Baal Shem Tov believed that the blasts represent our tears, expressing the deep emotion we feel each time we hear the shofar's call. One thing is certain—one warning blast is not enough. The shofar must be blown many times to rouse us from our walking slumber and demand our full attention.

Menaḥem Mendl of Kotzk taught that God can hear a cry of sorrow even when it is not uttered. We, too, can hear our own small voice, the cry of our heart, even over the trumpeting blare of the shofar. All we need is the courage to say, *"Heneini"*—"I am finally here, God. I know I have to change. And I am ready. Do what you will with me." Such self-abdication is difficult for most of us, but often, as some of our teachers have taught, we come to realize that all that stands between God and each of us is our blind "I."

The call to change is heard from many directions.

Tishrei 3

Cast away from yourselves all your transgressions, and create within yourselves a new heart and new spirit.

[Ezek. 18:31]

On Rosh Hashanah afternoon, we performed the ceremony of *"tashlikh"*—casting our sins into a stream or lake. Today we continue casting away our sins in other ways. That is the task assigned us on these *aseret y'mei t'shuvah*—these ten days of repentance.

Rabbi Israel Salanter taught that we have two eyes for a reason. With one eye, we look at our neighbors, fastening our gaze on their goodness, excellence, and most desirable qualities, while refraining from criticism, slander, and gossip. With the other eye, we turn inward to see our own weaknesses, imperfections, and shortcomings so we can correct them.

It may seem difficult to maintain our normal routine at this time of year. But that's one of the functions of the Jewish calendar—to wrestle us away from our accustomed pattern of living. Jewish tradition teaches us how to build a holy life for ourselves and those around us.

D'var aḥer: The fall holidays seem endless. In the presence of the Infinite, however, there is no end in sight.

Holy living grows from a holy life.

I possess nothing but Torah.

[B. Yevamot 109b]

*W*hat do we truly possess? The intense probing of these ten days turns our attention inward. We turn away from the outside world that normally claims our attention and focus on what really matters. We think about *what* we have gained and *whom* we have lost during the past year. These thoughts may still hurt us. We may be scared. Life can be so uncompromising! We ask ourselves what we achieved through all these pursuits. We despair: perhaps many of our strivings were in vain!

*B*ut we have an alternative to despair: Torah study. We can enter the gate of sacred study, a necessary step in our quest for sacred living. We must not hurry through the text. We need to drink in its sweetness, savor its taste. Sometimes we find sweetness in surprising places. So said the psalmist: ". . . with honey from the rock will I nurture you" (Psalm 81:17).

*O*nce someone went to a rabbi, searching for answers to certain difficult questions. Said the seeker, "I have already been through the entire Torah. I have not found the answers to my questions in it." The rabbi responded, "You may indeed have been through the entire Torah, but has the entire Torah been through you?"

Torah is an eternal possession.

Tishrei 5

All come to grief through lashon ha-ra, the evil tongue.

[B. Bava Batra 165a]

*L*ashon ha-ra can be translated as gossip, slander, or simply speaking ill of another person. What makes it so insidious is that we often don't even realize we're guilty of it. We may offer a word, a comment, a story—nothing meant to hurt. Then one comment leads to another, and one person speaks to another, and pain is borne along with the words. Speak ill of no one; the pain you cause ultimately will be your own.

Rabbi Ḥaim of Brisk once recounted the following story: Once when travelling on a train, he shared a compartment with a group of people whose stylish clothing marked them as distinguished. The rabbi was modestly dressed, as was his custom. Throughout the trip, the well-dressed passengers made comments to one another, but never engaged the rabbi in conversation. He understood that they considered him, based on his dress, in a class far lower than their own. So they only talked *about* him, whispering to one another during the entire train ride. When the train arrived in Brisk, travellers noticed that a huge crowd gathered to greet the train. When the throng embraced Rabbi Ḥaim, his travelling companions ran up to him and begged his forgiveness. "We didn't realize who you were!" The rabbi cautioned them, "You need not ask forgiveness of me. Request forgiveness of the many good people you thought I was." We, too, must beg *m'hila* of all those people whom we ignore when we pass them on the street, thinking them beneath us. In their midst, the Messiah might be securing shelter from the cold.

The Messiah hides in each and every one of us.

Tishrei 6

If you have committed many misdeeds, then do many mitzvot to match them.

[Leviticus Rabbah 21:1]

Transforming misdeeds into *mitzvot* is one of the most amazing effects of *t'shuvah*. Even more wondrous is the transformation of the one who committed the wrongdoing in the first place. As human beings, we invariably struggle and sin. Then we have to work hard at forgiveness. But we can and do change, evolving into better people. Had we not sinned in the first place, perhaps we would not now be ready to do *t'shuvah* and turn our whole life in God's direction. Performing *mitzvot* can help us to heal. Not only do *mitzvot* rebuild relationships between individuals and God, but they also repair broken relationships between people. They provide us with divine instructions for holy living.

Where and how we begin doing *mitzvot* does not matter. What matters is that we begin now. This week. Before Yom Kippur. We can involve our friends and members of our family. We can teach others (especially our children if we have them) by doing *mitzvot* rather than by just talking about them. Doing *mitzvot* with others often brings people together in ways we can never anticipate nor duplicate. And through our efforts we can change the world, one redeeming act at a time. As we pray during this season, *t'shuvah, t'fillah,* and *tzedakah* indeed can thwart the severity of the decree. We need not worry about everything. We can leave that to God. There are plenty of little things broken in the world. All we have to do is pick *one* of them and begin to fix it.

T'shuvah, t'fillah, **and** *tzedakah* **can change our world.**

Tishrei 7

You [can and] shall return.

[Deut. 30:2]

*T*he High Holy Days season is colored by many themes. We are
dazzled each day by its spectrum of emotions. Perhaps the most
powerful theme during this period is the constancy of hope. No matter
where we are, what we do, or what has happened to us, our profound
belief in tomorrow is implicit in our every thought this time of year. We
don't always understand why or from where this faith in the future
comes, but we know it is there. We taste it each week on Shabbat, especially at twilight as Shabbat is about to leave us. We experience it now
as we prepare for the awesome climax of Yom Kippur. It is the messian-
ic impulse, to experience what our tradition sometimes calls "the end of
days." Ironically, we get to that end time by turning backward rather
than by going forward. We get there through *t'shuvah.*

Sometimes we feel alone, isolated, or estranged. No matter how hard
we try, we can't seem to get a foothold in the world. We fear that
nobody wants anything to do with us. Perhaps we don't realize how far
we have run from *them!* We can return. Acknowledging this simple
truth can make the difference between a holy life and a lonely one.

Return requires work on our part. We can't just wait for something to
happen. Leon de Modena once said, "Words are the guides to acts. The
mouth makes the first move." During this special week between Rosh
Hashanah and Yom Kippur, especially on Shabbat Shuvah (the Sabbath
of Return), turn back. It's the only way to move forward toward the End
of Days.

To return only requires that we take one step in the other direction.

> *Adonai, Adonai, God, merciful and gracious,*
> *long-suffering and abundant in goodness and*
> *truth, keeping mercy unto the thousandth*
> *generation, forgiving iniquity, transgression*
> *and sin.*
>
> [Exod. 34:6–7]

*T*hese thirteen qualities or attributes of God that have become part of the High Holy Days liturgy are taken directly from the Torah. Although they are recited at various times throughout the year, they are particularly poignant when recited on this eighth day of Tishrei, according to the tradition of Rabbi Amittai ben Shefatiah, who lived around 900 C.E. Rabbi Amittai taught that these words demand all our attention during these ten days, especially today, because the next evening is Kol Nidre. As we meditate upon these thirteen measures of divine compassion, we constantly should remember what the rabbis teach in the midrash: The Holy Blessed One reaches out to us during this period and promises, "My hands reach out to the penitent, turning back no one who gives me his [or her] heart in *t'shuvah*" (Psalms Rabbah 120:7).

Rabbi Israel Salanter taught that our entire life is the result of God's mercy, but we often remain blind to the many miracles that surround us. They simply pass us by, because we are busy looking for them in the wrong places. We take for granted that the precious life entrusted to us—until it is threatened. We need to learn to live each day as if it is our last and to pray that it not be!

We learn a sobering lesson through the observance of these holy days: by miracles we indeed survive, but miracles may not happen everyday.

Each experience of God is a different revelation.

Tishrei 9

Light is sown for the righteous and joy for the honest of heart.

[Ps. 97:11]

*T*his text from the Psalms is sung often in the synagogue, but when we sing it during the Torah processional on Erev Yom Kippur, the words take on a totally new meaning. Who are the righteous who alone receive divine light? If I am truly honest with myself and others, can I too reach such a state of joy? As we attain spiritual maturity, we come to realize that not everyone achieves divine illumination. However, we can all bathe in divine light. To receive that light, however, we must be willing to open our hearts to it. If we fear that we cannot, we can ask for help: "Adonai Your God will open your heart and your children's hearts . . . for the purpose of giving you life" (Deuteronomy 30:6).

The Maggid of Dubno once told this story: Once a visitor came to a foreign city in the middle of the night. He was aroused from his slumber by a loud noise. When he queried his host, the visitor was told that this noise was a warning to the town's inhabitants that there was a fire in their midst. The visitor then went back to sleep. When he arose the next day, he discovered that somehow the fire had been extinguished. He had failed to understand that the alarm was a summons for help, alerting those responsible for fighting fires in the city. Foolishly, the visitor had thought that the alarm itself was sufficient to extinguish the fire.

Like the visitor in the Maggid's story, some people may not understand how t'shuvah works. We must sound the alarm for them. Then we must pray that we hear it as well.

Only when the ears hear can the heart receive divine light.

Tishrei 10 —Yom Kippur

*On this day atonement shall be made for you
to cleanse yourself from all the sins; you shall
be clean before Adonai Your God.*

[Lev. 16:30]

*A*s promised, this is the day for which you have been waiting
and working: *Yom Hakippurim*, literally, the day of *many*
atonements. Although our days generally move rapidly—more so as we
age—we discover that today time stands still as we rise before God in
prayer. Past and present rush forward to embrace the future. In a meta-
physical sense, we die on Yom Kippur. We leave behind our former
selves, praying, "May my death be an expiation for all my sins"
(Sanhedrin 6:2). Rabbi Abraham Joshua Heschel put it this way: "We
are all failures. At least one day a year we should recognize it."

After so much spiritual work, we feel totally spent. Such psychic
exhaustion is expected, especially as we drain our physical strength by
fasting. In our struggle to spend these last moments repairing our relationship with the Almighty and saving ourselves, we may become
tongue-tied. The liturgy just doesn't work. Prayers stick in our throats,
powerless to express what we feel in the depths of our hearts.

The Baal Shem Tov once assured a repentant person who was returning
to Judaism in adulthood that reciting the alphabet before God would be
sufficient. Our words of repentance too will open God's heart.

The words of repentance forge their own path
into our soul, and into God's heart.

Moving to Sukkot and Beyond

Yom Kippur may be over, but the work of spiritual self-repair is never complete. There are always loose ends, goals yet to be accomplished. And as we lead our lives, our world continues to change, as do our relationships with others. The world is in motion and so is our dynamic relationship with it. That's why Hoshanah Rabbah (the day before Shemini Atzeret and Simḥat Torah at the end of the Sukkot festival) comes only days after Yom Kippur, providing us with an additional opportunity for t'shuvah. The rabbis never want us to think it is too late to return to God. And God is always prepared to welcome us back.

One rabbinic parable tells of a sovereign ruler (God) whose adult child (us) decides to leave the protective confines of the palace to try to make it on his own. After travelling a great distance, he is ready to come home, but finds himself without the means to do so. The young prince sends word to the king, asking that he come to him. The king replies, "If you can find the way to travel half the distance, I will help you find the rest of your way home."

The message is clear: God wants to help us do t'shuvah and even will provide us with the means to make the journey. However, we must be willing to go half the distance on our own. The first steps of any journey may be the most difficult, but they are also the most important. Look, for instance, at the Exodus from Egypt. How many times were our ancestors ready to return to slavery because the desert journey became too tough? Desert journeys are difficult. Eventually, however, the Israelites reached the promised land. We can, too!

Some rabbis suggest that we have until Hanukkah to finish making amends. That's when things seem darker than at any other time of year. But the theme of return extends even beyond this period, running throughout the Jewish calendar year. Rabbi Lawrence Hoffman teaches that the full range of human emotions manifest themselves in different ways throughout the holiday cycle. We move through them all in readiness to return during the awesome High Holy Days. Thus, each year when Rosh Hashanah returns once again, we feel totally spent.

Moses Maimonides, the Rambam, had another way of looking at it. He said, "It is necessary that all people, throughout the year, should regard themselves as if half-innocent and half-guilty. . . . Thus, if they commit one sin, they press down on the scale of guilt against themselves. If they do one *mitzvah,* they turn the scale of merit in their favor" (*Hilkhot T'shuvah* 3:8).

Inspired by this High Holy Days season, many of us promise ourselves to become more active in institutional Jewish life, and we make commitments to ourselves for the coming year. The music touches us. The rabbi's words motivate us. The cantor's songs elevate our souls. So we say to ourselves and members of our family, "We're going to do more this year. Let's go to services more often. Let's study regularly. And let's finally get involved with a *tzedakah* project of some kind." Sometimes we honor these commitments. Too often, however, we let them lapse.

Living a holy life is not easy, but it's the only way we can become whole. The Jewish ritual of this season is structured to help us begin living that holy life. We can act on our renewed commitment to Judaism as soon as Yom Kippur is over by putting the first board of our sukkah in place. As we prepare to celebrate the natural harvest, we take note of the harvest of our lives. One rabbi suggests that the sequence of images embodied in these concrete rituals echoes the themes already familiar to us from our daily recitation of Psalm 27: Adonai becomes "our light" on Rosh Hashanah and "our salvation" on Yom Kippur, and literally "hides us in the tent" on Sukkot.

After all these fall holidays—how many there are!—we begin the long haul of the year. We have to return to the grind of daily living. How difficult it is for us, how we chafe under the repetitiveness of unending routine. These familiar patterns that we take for granted until they are disrupted, however, provide us with stability in an often rocky world. We could not sustain a steady diet of holy days. The Jewish calendar seasons our routine with sacred moments, helping us to find meaning and purpose in our complicated and sometimes fractured lives. Throughout the year, we find respite from our work on Shabbat, a day of sheer delight, when we need not work at all.

In the Jewish calendar, there are endless opportunities to live spiritual lives. Six weeks after Hanukkah, for example, comes Tu b'Shevat, the New Year of the Trees, falling between mid-January and mid-February. Here, in the heart of winter, we celebrate the first stirrings of spring, catching a glimpse, as we do, of the mystery of the natural order. We set our inner spirits free on Purim and savor our hard-won freedom as a people on Passover. Then we begin the counting of the Omer, preparing ourselves for revelation fifty days later on Shavuot. In the middle of this period of antic-ipation come Yom Hashoah (Holocaust Memorial Day), Yom Ha-atzmaut (Israel's Independence Day), and finally Shavuot, which celebrates the giv-ing of Torah on Sinai during our journey from Egypt to Canaan. And in the middle of summer, we recall the endless cycle of destruction marking Jewish history by setting aside one day, Tisha b'Av (the ninth of the month of Av), to remember the darkness, hoping thereby to lift its long shadow from the remainder of our year. Throughout this rich cycle of the Jewish calendar, we follow the pattern for personal renewal we established in our preparation for Rosh Hashanah and Yom Kippur. It works all year long.

*O*nce, the Maggid of Dubno, wanting to convince his fellow Jews to move beyond their High Holy Days Judaism (a phenomenon he, too, experi-enced in Europe two hundred years ago), told the following story on Rosh Hashanah to his congregants, most of whom did not frequent the syna-gogue on most other days of the year:

A local merchant lost his entire business and inventory in a fire. The merchant was worried about how he might pay his creditors since he had nothing left to sell. In particular, he worried about his chief supplier, a manufacturer who had sold him most of his goods for resale. When shar-ing this tale of woe with a friend, the friend suggested that the merchant go to the home of the supplier and tell him the whole story of the fire. "After all," he said, "you have been a good paying customer for many years. Your record is clean. Perhaps he will have pity on you and allow you to repay your debt as you rebuild your business."

So the merchant mustered up sufficient courage to go to his supplier's home. As he approached the doorstep, he broke down in tears. He could not go through with his plan. Upon hearing the merchant's cries, the supplier opened the door and asked, "What is the matter? Why are you here?" The merchant poured out his tale of woe, telling him all the details about the fire and about how terrible he felt not to be able to pay for the supplier's goods. The supplier replied, "Don't worry about your debt. You have been a good customer for years. Not only will I forgive you the debt, but I will also lend you the money to help you get started once again." And then he sent the merchant on his way.

As the merchant retold the story to his friend, a neighbor overheard the exchange. He thought to himself, "Maybe if I try the same thing, I can get that man to give me money, too." So he went to the home of the merchant's supplier and forced his tears. When the supplier opened the door, the stranger told him a story similar to the one that the merchant had told. Yet this time, the supplier rebuked him, refusing even to listen to the whole story. Puzzled, the stranger recounted the story of the merchant. The supplier replied, "I know that man. I have had a business relationship with him for many years. We have become friends. I don't know you at all. With you, there is nothing." The Maggid said to his congregants. "It's the same thing with God. It takes time to develop a relationship. We can't expect it overnight. It must be nurtured throughout the year."

So, as we part ways to enter the new year, let's commit ourselves to maintain a dialogue with God. Continue the process of *ḥeshbon hanefesh,* the personal accounting of our soul. Probe deeply. Forsake the sins we have committed and ask forgiveness of those we have wronged. Vow not to sin again, and then avoid the circumstances that may have led us there in the first place. Confess our sins before God. And pray that we all might be forgiven.

May we find our hearts prepared to do *t'shuvah* and emerge renewed.

Teachers and Their Texts

Baal Shem Tov (1700–1760): literally "Master of the Good Name," the popular name of Israel ben Eliezer; also called the Besht, he founded the hasidic movement.

Levi Yitzhak of Berditchev (ca., 1740–1810): hasidic rabbi known for his theological hutzpah in the midst of his community; founder of Hasidism in central Poland, a movement that he consolidated in Lithuania and furthered in the Ukraine.

Eugene B. Borowitz (1924–): leading contemporary liberal Jewish theologian whose work focuses on authority and autonomy in decision-making and whose covenant theology reflects the relationship between an individual and God.

Nahman of Bratzlav (1772–1811): also spelled Breslov, he was known for his spiritual insights into Torah and Jewish tradition. He was also the great grandson to the Baal Shem Tov.

Haim Soloveichik of Brisk (1853–1918): also called Brest-Litovsk, he was head of the yeshivah at Volozhin before moving to Brisk to become its community rabbi.

Jonah of Gerona (ca. 1200–1263): author of *Sha-arei T'shuvah* and father of Musar movement, which emphasizes virtues and piety through ethics.

Glükel of Hameln (1645–1724): German Jewish woman whose *Memoirs* contain rare insights into the human condition, particularly from the perspective of a woman.

Yose ben Halafta (middle second century C.E.): community leader after the Bar Kokhba rebellion.

Judah Halevi (before 1075–1141): medieval Jewish poet/philosopher whose writings reflect his travels in Spain and elsewhere.

Jacob Moses Harlap (1883–1951): rabbi, talmudist, kabbalist. A disciple of Abraham Isaac Kook, he became rabbi of the Sha-arei Hesed district of Jerusalem in 1908 and taught in the Etz Hayyim Yeshivah. He later served as dean of Yeshivat Merkaz ha-Rav. His halakhic research was published in six volumes as *Beit Zevul*, and his work on Jewish thought was collected as *Mei Marom*.

Abraham Joshua Heschel (1907–1972): leading theologian who brought light to social problems through religious tradition; he sought to rediscover the religious dimension in life that might permit a divine encounter to take place.

Lawrence Hoffman (1942–): leading contemporary liberal Jewish liturgist who applies systems theory to Jewish worship.

Abraham Isaac Kook (1865–1935): first Ashkenazic chief rabbi of Palestine. His writings reflect a leaning toward mysticism.

Menahem Mendl of Kotzk (1787–1859): hasidic teacher known for his unyielding pursuit of truth.

Lawrence Kushner (1943–): leading contemporary proponent and teacher of Jewish spiritual renewal in the Reform movement.

Isaac Luria (1534–1572): called the ARI, he was a mystic who made his way to Safed, Israel, where he schooled his disciples in a mysticism that taught communion with God was possible through techniques of intense concentration.

Maggid of Dubno (1741–1804): the popular name of Jacob Kranz, a wandering preacher and teller of tales who spoke in parables so that all might understand his message.

Moses ben Maimon (1135–1204): usually called Mamonides or the Rambam, one of the great thinkers in Jewish history. Trained as an Aristotelian, he was best known for his philosophical *Guide to the Perplexed* and legal *Mishneh Torah*.

Leon de Modena (1571–1648): Judah Aryeh, alternatively Leone Modena, Italian Jewish scholar.

Israel Salanter (1810–1883): Israel ben Zev Wolf, founder of the Musar movement (Jewish guidance for ethical behavior).

Amittai ben Shefatiah (late ninth century): liturgical poet in southern Italy.

Joseph B. Soleveitchik (1903–1993): known as the "Rav," he was the foremost proponent of modern Orthodoxy, blending classic halakhic Judaism with modern American culture.

T'khine of the Matriarchs: prayers in Yiddish by women, probably published in Lvov, Poland, in 1796.

Andrea Weiss (1965–): contemporary Reform rabbi.

Rabbi Yitzhak (middle second century): known primarily for his exegesis in non-talmudic sources.

Glossary

Amos: eighth century prophet who considered righteousness the most important moral attribute.

beg(ging) *m'hila:* asking for forgiveness in preparation for atonement.

bein hashamashot: literally "between the suns," this term refers to twilight, when things are difficult to see and are clouded in mystery; the rabbis determined that many of the miracles of the Bible were created in the last moments before the first Shabbat of Creation.

b'tzelem Elohim: literally "in the image of God," this term refers to human beings.

Elul: the sixth Hebrew month, which occurs in late summer (late August to early September), known for its theme of introspection.

Ezra: one of two great leaders who led the return to Israel from Babylonian captivity in the sixth century B.C.E.

Hanukkah: the festival of lights, which begins on the 25th of Kislev (usually in late November or December), celebrates the religious freedom earned through the Hasmoneans' defeat of the Assyrian-Greek forces in 164 B.C.E.

havdalah: ceremony held after sunset that distinguishes a holy day (particularly Shabbat) from other days.

heshbon hanefesh: literally "an accounting of the soul," this term refers to introspection.

High Holy Days: the collective name for the fall Holy Days, referring specifically to Rosh Hashanah and Yom Kippur.

Hoshanah Rabbah: a holiday that is part of the Sukkot festival, it starts on the eve of the seventh day and is punctuated with processionals and chants of *"hoshanah"* ("save us").

kavannah (pl. kavannot): literally "intention," this term generally refers to short sacred phrases or words used to help prepare a person for prayer or study and often is used by mystics as a Jewish mantra.

Kol Nidrei: the leitmotif prayer on the evening of Yom Kippur that annuls all vows.

lashon ha-ra: literally "evil tongue," this term refers generally to gossip and the spreading of rumors.

Musar: Jewish moral teaching, a movement founded by Rabbi Israel Salanter in the 19th century.

Nehemiah: a governor of Judea (fifth century B.C.E.), who is remembered especially for his devotion to social reformation.

nehemta: literally "consolation," a literary technique traditionally employed by rabbis at the end of sermons and haftarah readings.

Neilah: the final service of Yom Kippur.

Omer: the period of counting from the second day of Passover (and deliverance from slavery) until Shavuot (and the revelation of Torah), a span of seven weeks.

Purim: the late winter festival (in February or March) that marks the occasion when the ancient Jews of Persia were saved from destruction.

reah nihoah: literally "pleasing smoke," this term refers to the fragrant smoke that arose from the Temple altar during a sacrifice.

Rosh Hashanah: the New Year holiday, which initiates the intensive period of introspection on the first of Tishrei (from early September to October).

selihot: penitential prayers, recited particularly during Elul and Tishrei.

Shabbat Shuvah: the Sabbath of Return that falls between Rosh Hashanah and Yom Kippur.

Shavuot: the spring festival that marks the giving of Torah on Sinai (late May to early June).

Shemini Atzeret: the concluding festival of assembly on the last day of Sukkot.

sh'varim: one of the shofar blasts, noted for its broken tones.

Simhat Torah: holiday celebrating the beginning and ending of the Torah reading cycle at the end of Sukkot.

Song of Songs: one of the five biblical scrolls. An erotic love poem, interpreted as an allegory expressing the love between God and the Jewish people.

Sukkot: the fall festival of booths, which commemorates the temporary dwellings of the Israelites during the journey in the desert.

t'fillah: prayer, liturgy.

Tisha b'Av: late summer commemoration that marks the destruction of the ancient temples in Jerusalem as well as other catastrophes in Jewish history.

Tishrei: fall month that includes the High Holy Days.

t'kiah: one of the shofar blasts, noted for its long continuous tone.

t'ruah: one of the shofar blasts, noted for its series of staccato tones.

t'shuvah: repentance, return, and renewal.

Tu b'Shevat: midwinter festival that celebrates rebirth and renewal, especially of nature and trees (in late January to early February); also known as the New Year of the Trees.

tzedakah: acts of righteousness through charitable giving.

yetzer harah: literally "the inclination to do evil"; also refers to natural, libidinal drives.

Yom Ha-atzmaut: Israel Independence Day, which occurs in the spring.

Yom Hashoah: Holocaust Memorial Day, which occurs one week before Yom Ha-atzmaut.

Yom Kippur: Day of Atonement, which occurs in the fall on the tenth of Tishrei.